WILDCATS

Mountain Lions

by Erika L. Shores
Consulting Editor: Gail Saunders-Smith, PhD

Consultant: Robin Keith
Senior Research Coordinator
San Diego Zoo's Institute for Conservation Research

CAPSTONE PRESS
a capstone imprint

Pebble Plus is published by Capstone Press,
151 Good Counsel Drive, P.O. Box 669, Mankato, Minnesota 56002.
www.capstonepub.com

Books published by Capstone Press are manufactured with paper containing at least 10 percent post-consumer waste.

Library of Congress Cataloging-in-Publication Data
Shores, Erika L., 1976–
Mountain lions / by Erika L. Shores.
p. cm.—(Pebble plus. Wildcats)
Includes bibliographical references and index.
Summary: "Simple text and full-color photos explain the habitat, life cycle, range, and behavior of mountain lions"—Provided by publisher.
ISBN 978-1-4296-4485-3 (library binding)
1. Puma—Juvenile literature. I. Title. II. Series.
QL737.C23S5457 2011
599.75'24—dc22 2010002799

Editorial Credits
Katy Kudela, editor; Bobbie Nuytten, designer; Svetlana Zhurkin, media researcher; Eric Manske, production specialist

Photo Credits
Alamy/Petra Wegner, 16–17
Getty Images/Robert Harding World Imagery/James Hager, cover, 9; Visuals Unlimited/Joe McDonald, 11
iStockphoto/Davina Graham, back cover, 13; Tom Tietz, 19
Shutterstock/Dennis Donohue, 5, 14–15, 21; ecliptic blue, 1; Fenton (paw prints), cover and throughout;
Ronnie Howard, 7

The author dedicates this book to her son, Edison Michael Shores.

Note to Parents and Teachers

The Wildcats series supports national science standards related to life science. This book describes and illustrates mountain lions. The images support early readers in understanding the text. The repetition of words and phrases helps early readers learn new words. This book also introduces early readers to subject-specific vocabulary words, which are defined in the Glossary section. Early readers may need assistance to read some words and to use the Table of Contents, Glossary, Read More, Internet Sites, and Index sections of the book.

Printed in the United States of America in North Mankato, Minnesota.
012011 006047R

Table of Contents

A Wildcat with Many Names

Mountain lions are named
for the rocky cliffs
where they live.
They are also called pumas,
cougars, and panthers.

Mountain lions also live
in forests and deserts.
They prowl North
and South America.

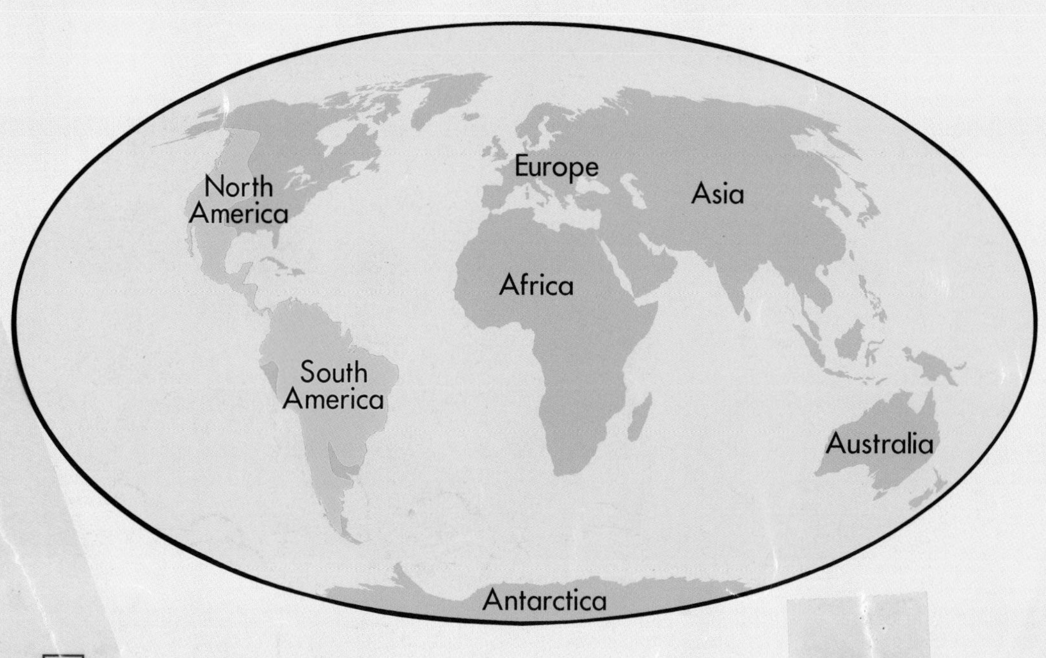

where mountain lions live

Mountain Lion Bodies

Mountain lions are large.
These wildcats grow
up to 7 feet (2 meters) long.
They weigh up to 260 pounds
(118 kilograms).

Mountain lions have
short, thick fur.
Their tan color helps them
blend in with rocky cliffs.

Hunting Prey

Mountain lions hunt
at dawn and at dusk.
They stalk deer,
elk, and rabbits.

A mountain lion can leap
30 feet (9 m) to catch prey.
The hungry cat uses its strong
paws and sharp claws
to bring down an animal.

Mountain Lion Life Cycle

Most mountain lions mate
in winter and early spring.
Females make crying sounds
to attract males.
These cries sound like screams.

Female mountain lions
give birth to litters
of one to six kittens.
Brown spots cover
the kittens' fuzzy, soft fur.

After 18 months, young cats
are ready to live on their own.
They have learned to hunt.
Mountain lions live
12 to 20 years in the wild.

Glossary

cliff—a high, steep rock face

dawn—the beginning of day; sunrise

dusk—the time of day after sunset when it is nearly dark

litter—a group of animals born at the same time to one mother

mate—to join together to produce young

prey—an animal hunted by another animal for food

prowl—to move around quietly and secretly

stalk—to hunt an animal in a quiet, secret way

Read More

Pitts, Zachary. *The Pebble First Guide to Wildcats.* Pebble First Guides. Mankato, Minn.: Capstone Press, 2009.

Rodriguez, Cindy. *Cougars.* Eye to Eye with Endangered Species. Vero Beach, Fla.: Rourke Pub. LLC, 2009.

Internet Sites

FactHound offers a safe, fun way to find Internet sites related to this book. All of the sites on FactHound have been researched by our staff.

Here's all you do:

Visit *www.facthound.com*

FactHound will fetch the best sites for you!

Index

Word Count: 180
Grade: 1
Early-Intervention Level: 17